THIRTEEN "13"

Kelvin Page Jr.
Thirteen "13"

Published by Spines
ISBN: 979-8-89383-350-8

THIRTEEN "13"

KELVIN PAGE JR.

FOREWORD

Before anything, I just want to thank God for shutting me in and pushing me out of my comfort zone. I've sacrificed SOOO much. While being silenced simultaneously. This body of work was not written for profit by any means. This was solely written as therapy for self. The concept of each section, came by way of prayer, fasting and meditation. I only wrote once I was in God's presence. I've never been vulnerable on this scale before. BUT GOD...! I cried both tears of joy and deep pain while writing this material.

With that being said, I give a HUGE thank you to each of you who chose to purchase and actually read my first book. Special shout out to my parents, my inner circle (Lexi/Amaya, OB & Brittany), my spiritual parents, Pastor B & PK and of course Radical City!!! Every text message, FaceTime, voice memo, zoom meeting, and time spent together has broken me down and slowly but surely piece my broken heart together. YOU ALL have helped save me from causing my own downfall. Truly invaluable, y'all are to me. I owe you everything!!!

You're probably wondering why this book is titled the number "Thirteen." Over the past few years, I've noticed that several of my milestones or significant occurrences have the number 13 associated with them. Life is about patterns and there's a consistent pattern of this very number showing up each time. I never seek it. If a situation occurs, I see the number(s) and I'll be surprised. Although I'm aware of numerology, the science of numbers, I don't worship it. Needless to say, here's a list to give you further insight:

1. My first car passed state inspection in April 2013.

2. My first day of college was 13 days after high school graduation.

3. The address of the house I grew up in is 904. 9+4=13.

4. My favorite shirt that I've had for years now has Isaiah 41:13 on it.

5. Something spiritually strange always happens on Friday the 13th. The strangest of them all is when I was 16 years old, walking to school. A random car with 2 guys pulled on me at a red light and asked me did I wanna go for a ride. The guy in the passenger seat, while having his chair leaned back, looked me dead in the eyes and aggressively shook his head saying "no" with a scared look on his face. I chuckled, told em "Nah. I'm good" and kept walking. Homeboy really tried to kidnap in broad day light.

6. Upon my return to Baltimore, I started a new job on July 13th 2022.

7. 9/13/2022

Pastor B gave me his mantle, anointed me with his healing abilities (only person other than his natural son), and all of his favor.

8. 12/13/2022

Ordered iPhone 13. PK tasked me to conduct the Thursday midnight prayer call where I preached my first sermonette. Also, Pastors commanded M.I.T. to prepare a 3 minute sermonette for next months class.

9. 11/09/2023

Went to the MVA to get hard plates. Statewide network issue. Rescheduled for 11/13/23. Picked up hard plates w/ temp tags & registration.

10. 4/9/2024 (4+9=13)

Pastor B pulled me into the Leaders Lounge and invited me back to MIT.

What does all of this have to do with this book? I truly believe God gave me the command to pen this body of work as an indicator of a paradigm shift in the realm of the spirit for my generation. In layman's terms, times are changing. Inflation, the seasons, mental health, technology and honorable mentions to my lower back and knee caps lol. In all seriousness, this shift isn't just about the negative effects but also that God is raising up a new generation of generals in the spirit and world leaders. This generation has its own way of thinking and operating in life. Some of us are lost with little to no guidance. While others study generations before us and made adjustments along the way while keeping core principles and morals in tact. What's peculiar about this is that a portion of younger and elderly folks don't get along. Why? Because the young group thinks they know it all due to the impact of technological advancements. While the older group has more experience in this thing called life. Both of which, are stubborn and don't like to be wrong. Major disconnect! Simple but challenging solution....be quiet and take notes from each other. Older people are trash with the technology that they've been forced to adapt to due to new societal norms. Bless their souls! Young folks can help with that. Although, technology has advanced greatly, foundational life lessons are still the same from ages ago. How to treat people, how to conduct yourself in different scenarios, how to survive & thrive in life, etc. This is where the older folks can give wisdom and insight when applicable.

Therefore, allow my journal entries turned book material, bridge that gap between the older and younger groups. I believe anybody who lays their eyes on this material will walk away with something positive. No matter how big or small. Prayerfully, you enjoy the ride. Be well.

PART I

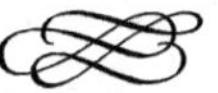

ONE

"Thought One"

"I'm not in the convincing business. I'm in the faith business. Why? Cause faith is the currency of Heaven. So, I stand on my Father's business!" -Yours truly

At some point in your life, you have to get to a point where you understand the difference between convincing and conversing. Yes, you can convince somebody while conversing with them but an authentic conversation doesn't call for emphasized persuasion. Stick with me!

For example, in a relationship, you shouldn't have to persuade somebody to stay with you if they're sabotaging it. Let them leave. Better yet, show them the way out and wish them well. In the same breath, if we're having an organic discussion about fruit, I suppose, it's healthy to exchange info about which fruit has what benefits that help your particular health concerns. No persuasion is needed. A healthy banter at best.

We walk by faith, not by sight (2 Corinthians 5:7)

TWO

"Believe"

Father, I believe but help my unbelief (Mark 9:24)

In my tender 30 years of living, I've noticed that while walking this walk with Christ, God gives me visions that don't reflect what's in my bank account, intellect, or current circle of influence. A wise man once told me, "If your dreams don't scare you, they aren't big enough."

At the age of 19, God gave me a vision of a man standing on this elegant stainless steel and translucent balcony attached to his mansion on a hill. He closed his eyes, inhaled, and exhaled slowly. Hearing footsteps he then looked back to his left and laid eyes on his beautiful melanated wife and daughter. All of them were wearing white. His heart was filled with purpose, joy, peace, and vigor. I woke up in my twin bed with a negative bank account living with my mother. Boy, was I pissed! I might've called God toxic for that stunt lol. Nonetheless, it was from that moment on I laid my suicidal thoughts to rest and became more intentional about purpose, health, and wealth.

See what I realize at this juncture is that most, if not all, of the visions and downloads God gives me that are about me won't make sense right away. Especially when you're in the thick of a transformation. It's scary and will cause intense doubt at times. You might even feel stuck or as if you're taking one step forward and three steps back. But no matter what, you have to P.U.S.H. (Pray Until Something Happens)! "Father, I believe. But help my unbelief."

I know it hurts. I know it's not pretty. It comes with the territory. The sleepless nights, crying when you're alone, mentally rehearsing trauma, rejection, death of loved ones, losing family and friends, friendship dynamics changing, loneliness, double-mindedness, health issues, and constantly asking God, "Why," "Is that you?" and/or "Is it really that deep?" Kids acting out more than normal, I'm sure. I can't relate to that one just yet, but I've definitely seen it. Trust me, I know! Nothing great comes easy. Welcome to the pruning! God will strip you of all things you take pride in and shut you in until you get to a point where you have the capacity to handle the responsibilities He WANTS to trust you with. Minimal room for error! YOU HAVE TO LOCK IN!!! I know you feel like nobody cares 'cause nobody calls to check on you or simply ask you, "Are you ok?" Or "Do you need anything?" I GET IT. "Father, I believe. But help my unbelief."

God still pulling on those heartstrings, isn't He? He's slowly but surely taking away your palate for those vices you've had for years now, isn't He? It's all a part of the process. Document your journey. Get a therapist. Some practices are ProBono. So you have no excuses. Whatever you do, KEEP GOING! Take time off. Take 5-10 dopamine breaks. Optimize your schedule. Schedule self. Spend more time with your inner child. They NEED you! Hug your loved ones more. Travel. Meditate. Whatever it takes. I don't care how many times life knocks you down. Cry, wipe your tears, stand to your feet, head up, chest out, back straight, and keep putting one foot in front of the other. "One day at a time" as the old folks say. "Father, I believe. But help my unbelief." It's okay to not be okay at times. But you have to keep going. Your family and friends need you! Your legacy needs you! Your inner child needs you! People are waiting for you to unlock some of their blessings because YOU are the key! God wants to use YOU and all of YOUR brokenness to be a blessing and beacon of light to others. You can't see it just yet so you don't believe it. But you do believe in Him. And THAT is all that matters.

THREE

"Thought Two"

"A jack of all trades is a master of none, but oftentimes better than a master of one" -Robert Greene, *Greene's Groat-Worth of Wit* (1952)

So many people use HALF of the above quote as an insult. To their ignorance and/or stupidity, the other half is the punchline. The entirety of the quote is words of admiration. Indulge and digest.

FOUR

"Download One"

The thing you're complaining about, somebody else is praying for. The thing you're praying about, somebody else is complaining about.

Solution: count your blessings daily and continue to work unto the Lord.

"Whatever you do, work at it with all your heart, as working for the Lord, not for human masters"

Colossians 3:23 (NIV)

"Give thanks in all circumstances; for this is God's will for you in Christ Jesus."

1 Thessalonians 5:18 (NIV)

FIVE

"Download Two"

In most cases, the people who "preach" heavily about humility and forgiveness are the main ones claiming "The Lord still working on me" when they get into with somebody. Especially, their loved ones. As my Pastor would say (@onlypastorB) "If you can't say amen, say ouch"

-forgiveness of the heart is what's key. It's letting that pain go with so much depth that it's no longer on your mind. Forgiveness is when you no longer mentally rehearse trauma. Forgiveness is setting or resetting boundaries. Most importantly, forgiveness IS FOR YOU, NOT THE OTHER PERSON!!!

"Bear with each other and forgive one another if any of you has a grievance against someone. Forgive as the Lord forgave you."

Colossians 3:13 (NIV)

SIX

"Ehh"

Roses are red

Violets are blue

If you don't like this book so far

Forget you lmbo

Now go to the next page and receive this blessing!

SEVEN

"Disappointment"

People admire you when you meet or exceed their expectations of you. But as soon as they see an inevitable imperfection, they write you off and you become a non-factor.

It's at this juncture when you need to have tunnel vision. This is the crossroads of purpose and pain. It's a sweet spot where God strategically places you and prunes you for the Kingdom.

Lock in. Keep your eyes on the prize and your foot on the gas. It's about the journey, not the destination.

EIGHT

"Díme"

Dímelo mami. Talk to me.

Tell me what's on your mind.

Keep your body to yourself cause I'm keeping mine.

This is a safe space. Don't let your past traumas dictate.

Your heart, to my ears

My courage, to your fears

Your protection is finally here

It's just you and I

The opinions of others, who cares?

The introspection of our inner kids

It's our language, our flow

We create it, as we go

Never perfect, through troubles we grow

The look in your eyes, lets me know

That little girl, just wants to glow

Stitches on your heart, yeah I know

Bobwire too, oh fa sho

What's the plan? Only God knows

Hold my hand. Don't let go

All we need is God. So let's go!

My love for you, unconditional

Deeply & undoubtably.

Ya tú sabé! Dímelo mami

(Dímelo means "talk to me" in Dominican Spanish. Be mindful, Dominican & Puerto Ricans speak Ebonics/slang)

NINE

"Sometimes"

Sometimes, I give my all and still fail.

I carefully feel,

for the fake love like I'm reading braille.

The disappointment & judgement I see in my loved ones eyes.

But I overlook it as if I'm blind

Duly noted. I adjust boundaries in real time

Fully aware that their problems with me, aren't mine

Doesn't matter. I love on em anyway.

Some people will never get it and that's ok.

I'm no better than them. I'm probably worse

I'm sure they have valid reasons for their disgust and low regard

Sometimes I, wonder what's the charge

Then again, what does it matter cause I'm just as flawed

I'm cognizant of the cuts & scars

Sometimes my mind is like a battlefield or prison bars

The damage is done.

Heal and move on.

TEN

"GPS Driver"

Follow the directions no matter what you see in front of you. Stick to the suggested route cause it is beyond your scope of vision. Most people use the GPS to prevent getting lost. Others use it for the fastest route with current traffic conditions. Thinking you know a better way, just to end up in more traffic. The GPS reroutes and still shows you the best way. Left. Right. Stop at the red light. Don't be hard-headed. Just obey. You'll get there right on time, today.

ELEVEN

As you're reading this, there's a systemic attack on men. Especially my melanated brothers, by way of the automotive industry. You guessed it right....the diabolical minivan! (I know you just made this face "😐" lol) Insanely functional and slightly attractive. Engineered with the entire family in mind, most makes offer aggressive and edgy sports packages to appeal more to male consumers. My good brothers, don't fall for it. Keep your dignity intact.

TWELVE

"Laugh A Little"

I started investing in stocks

Beef, chicken and vegetable

I hope one day I'll be a bouillonaire

-DockTok (Dad Joke)

Shout out to my grandma.

That's the only way she can hear

-@Dadsaysjokes

Why didn't juvenile get upset when his MacBook crashed?

He backed that thing up

-@alldefdadjokes

THIRTEEN

If you've gotten this far, prayerfully at least one section blessed you. A new perspective, a laugh, a tear or a sense of purpose and/or fulfillment. As long as you believe it was worth your time and money, I'm content with that. Either way I'm beyond grateful for taking time out of your busy day to completely read my first body of literary work. I appreciate you more than you know!

Quickly pray this prayer:

Father, you didn't have to wake me up today, but you chose fit to do so. This means I still have a purpose to fulfill. No matter what or how many darts life throws at me, may I retain an attitude of gratitude. Teach me the depths of YOUR unconditional love AND forgiveness. So that I may be a beacon of light to those I cross paths with. Especially the ones that get on my nerves. May you bless me and my village with wisdom, knowledge, insight and revelation. I thank you and love you Lord. Amen.

PART II

BOOK: PURPOSE & PASSION

CHAPTER ONE

"Humble Beginnings"

You pull up in your high-tech Eco-friendly drive way to your dream home in your dream car. As you put the car in park, take off your seat belt, and look in the rearview mirror, you adjust your clothes, grab your phone and keys, and press the engine stop button. You step out of the car, take a few steps and you find yourself standing there in awe. Gazing at the beauty of your property, you say to yourself, "Life's good but God is greater!" You walk to the front door, open it and suddenly you hear a buzzing sound. The sounds get louder and clearer. As you come to consciousness, you hit the button on your alarm clock. Laying there still trying to figure out where you are and how you got there, you realize you were dreaming! WHAT THE HECK!!! You realize you're in the bedroom of your mother's house. Upon this "epiphany" a grunting feeling of disappointment, depression and frustration comes across your heart. Back to reality. Looking around at your organized but small room, you think to yourself, "I've never seen or thought of such a thing in my life!" Sliding to the floor off the side of your bed and dropping to your knees, you pray to God.

"Father, I've never seen such a thing in my life. I'm broke, living paycheck to paycheck, lonely and living with my mom! Why would you show me such a thing?!" A still small voice says in return, "If you work hard enough, through you, I will build wealth for the next four generations of your family." In response, "But who am I? The lifestyle I live now is completely contrary to the person and lifestyle in that dream." "Have faith and faint not! You are not alone for I am always with you." Yes Lord.

In these moments of uncertainty, we as humans beings, full of emotions, become flustered. The realm of not knowing is a scary place for us. In an era full of instant gratification, we want our needs, desires and dreams met immediately. Unfortunately, it doesn't happen over night. Yes, your needs or daily essentials are to be provided regularly. However, your goals and dreams takes time. Passion, love and most importantly discipline over an extended period of time will bring any goal or dream to life. The daily practices of such actions will increase your faith. Faith is simply defined as believing beyond seeing. I urge you to never allow your current circumstances to dictate your future. If you want to lose weight, find a diet that works for you and your situation along with exercise 3-4 days a week and I guarantee you, you'll see results in 30 days or less. If you're looking to increase your income, identify your income-producing activities, increase those efforts and you'll see results within 30-90 days regardless of the industry. Keep in mind the reason and/or purpose why you began your endeavors. Visualize the outcome. This is one way to begin with the end in mind. These daily practices are detrimental to your success.

I've gained this wisdom and knowledge through my relationship with God, experience and wise words from others. It's crazy how time unveils certain events! Quite audacious my faith has become over the years. I was exposed to mental toughness early on because it runs in my family. Take a seat and ride with me through my verbal adventure as I share with you how it all began!

Growing up, my mom, my sister and I always lived with my grandparents, 2 uncles and 1 cousin. Two more uncles of mine stayed there too. They were always in the streets so they were rarely there. My fifth and oldest uncle owned his own house where he raised his daughter and oldest son. They lived with him. His baby boy, young Jo, was in foster care. My mom went to school to learn how to become a foster parent. She dreamed of taking custody of young Jo. That's a different story though!

TO BE CONTINUED!!

GOTCHA (Kanye voice)